EXTREME MACHINES

TRUCKS

IAN GRAHAM

W
FRANKLIN WATTS

This edition 2009

First published in 2006 by
Franklin Watts
338 Euston Road
London NW1 3BH

Franklin Watts Australia
Level 17/207 Kent Street
Sydney, NSW 2000

EXTREME MACHINES: TRUCKS
Created for Franklin Watts by
Q2A Creative
Editor: Chester Fisher
Designer: Sudakshina Basu
Picture Researcher: Jyoti Sethi

A CIP catalogue record for this book is available from the British Library.

ISBN 978 0 7496 8952 0

Printed in China

Dewey number: 629.224

Franklin Watts is a division of Hachette Children's Books, an Hachette Livre UK company.
www.hachettelivre.co.uk

PICTURE CREDITS

Front cover: Western Star Trucks Back cover: STRANA
pp. 1 main (Kenworth), 4 bottom (National Motor Museum, Beaulieu), 5 top (Alan Nash www.steam-up.co.uk),
5 bottom (National Motor Museum, Beaulieu), 6 bottom (The Sparwood and District Chamber of Commerce),
7 top (Liebherr Holding GmbH), 8 bottom (Photos courtesy of Mack Trucks, Inc. All rights reserved.), 9 top (The
Mack Trucks Historical Museum), 9 middle (Kenworth), 10 middle (Terex-Demag GmbH & Co.KG),11 bottom
(Liebherr Holding GmbH), 12-13 bottom (Oshkosh Truck Corporation),13 top (U.S. Army Photo By: Kimberly Lee),
13 bottom (BIGFOOT 4X4, Inc.),14 bottom (Kenworth), 15 middle (NASA), 15 right (NASA) 16 top (Peterbilt),
17 middle (Kenworth), 18 top (Western Star Trucks), 19 middle (Tim Ahlborn) 20 bottom (Adam Alberti),
21 top (Oshkosh Truck Corporation), 22 top (Nate Mecha), 23 top (STRANA), 23 bottom (STRANA),
24 top (BIGFOOT 4X4, Inc.), 25 bottom (BIGFOOT 4X4, Inc.), 26 bottom (National Motor Museum, Beaulieu),
27 top (DaimlerChrysler), 28 middle left (National Motor Museum, Beaulieu), 28 top right (National Motor
Museum, Beaulieu), 29 middle left (National Motor Museum, Beaulieu), 29 middle right
(National Motor Museum, Beaulieu), 29 bottom (National Motor Museum, Beaulieu).

CONTENTS

CURIOUS CARRIERS

Trucks are road vehicles that move goods wherever they need to go. Nearly everything you can see around you was transported or delivered by a truck.

OUT IN THE COLD

Early trucks, like the 1903 Vabis, were very different from trucks today. They were a bit like farm carts, only with an engine and steering wheel at the front. Drivers sat in the open, so if it rained, they got soaking wet! In cold weather, they had to wrap up well to keep warm.

RATTLE AND ROLL

Trucks like the 1903 Vabis shook and rattled along the road, because they had poor springs and thin solid tyres. Tyres filled with air, called pneumatic tyres, made trucks a bit more comfortable by the 1920s.

Early trucks, like this 1903 Vabis, had wooden wheels.

1903 VABIS

ENGINE	2-cylinder petrol
POWER	9 horsepower (hp)
LOAD CARRIED	1.5 tonnes (3,300 lb)
TOP SPEED	12 kph (7.5 mph)

STEAMING ALONG

Today, trucks are powered by diesel engines, but the first trucks were steam-powered. A steam engine used fire to heat a boilerful of water. The expanding steam made the engine go. Steam trucks were still being made in the 1920s. The Foden C-type was a popular British steam truck of that time, but it was one of the last steam trucks.

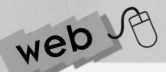

FINDER

http://www.scania.com/about/history
The history of Scania and Vabis trucks.
http://www.worldofsteam.com
Lots of information about steam trucks and other steam-powered vehicles.

1920s FODEN C-TYPE 'STEAMER'

ENGINE	Steam engine
POWER	23 hp
LOAD	6 tonnes (13,440 lb)
TOP SPEED	26 kph (16 mph)

The Foden C-type looked like a steam locomotive on the road.

MEGA TRUCKS

The world's biggest trucks are the giant earth haulers that work in mines. Some of them are as big as a house! They carry earth out of enormous holes in the ground where coal and other materials are mined.

TITAN

The biggest truck ever built was called the Terex Titan. Even when it was empty, it weighed as much as 175 cars. The Titan was built in 1978 and worked until 1990. Today it can be seen on display in the Canadian town of Sparwood, British Columbia.

LOCO POWER

The Terex Titan was powered by a railway locomotive engine, but the engine didn't drive the wheels! It was connected to a huge generator big enough to supply 250 homes with electricity. The generator ran four electric motors that drove the rear wheels.

Each of the Terex Titan's massive tyres weighs as much as three cars!

The T282 B is so big that the driver is only half the height of its giant wheels.

LIEBHERR T282 B

ENGINE	90-l (5,488 cu. in.) diesel
POWER	3,650 hp
EMPTY WEIGHT	229 tonnes (505,000 lb)
LOADED WEIGHT	592 tonnes (1,305,000 lb)

HEAVY HAULER

The Liebherr T282 B is the biggest earth-hauling truck in service today. It's a little smaller than the Terex Titan, but it can carry more than the Titan. Fully loaded, it holds up to 363 tonnes (800,000 lb) of earth. The driver's cab is so high that the driver has to climb up a long stairway to reach it. Each of these giant trucks costs about $3 million US.

TEREX TITAN

ENGINE	16-cylinder diesel
POWER	3,300 hp
EMPTY WEIGHT	235 tonnes (518,090 lb)
LOADED WEIGHT	549 tonnes (1,209,450 lb)

web

FINDER

http://www.sparwood.bc.ca/titaninf.htm
Information about the Terex Titan and a webcam to see it at work.
http://www.liebherr.com/me/en/40787.asp
Details of the Liebherr T282 truck.

EXTREME MACHINES Trucks

MATERIAL MOVERS

Buildings, bridges and roads are made from vast amounts of materials like concrete, bricks, steel, sand and gravel. Trucks transport these materials to construction sites.

CONCRETE MIXER TRUCKS

Most trucks can carry different cargoes, but some trucks are specially designed to carry one type of cargo. The concrete mixer truck is one of these special-purpose trucks. The Mack FDM700 is unusual. Most mixer trucks pour concrete out at the back. The FDM700 pours it out at the front.

DRUM AND BLADES

The drum is loaded with sand, gravel, cement and water. Then it spins to mix them up and make concrete. The drum has to keep moving to stop the concrete from setting hard. It has blades or paddles inside to keep everything churning around. To unload, the drum turns in the opposite direction. The blades push the concrete out of the drum and down a chute.

Lots of wheels spread the Mack FDM700s heavy weight.

MACK FDM700
CONCRETE MIXER TRUCK

ENGINE	12 litres (730 cu in) diesel
POWER	320 hp
WEIGHT	25-36 tonnes (56,000-80,000 lb)

TIPPER TRUCKS

Loose materials like sand and gravel are carried by road in tipper trucks like the Kenworth T800. When the truck finishes its journey, the driver tips up the back of the truck. The back swings open and all the sand or gravel slides out on to the ground.

One version of the sturdy Kenworth T800 is a tipper truck.

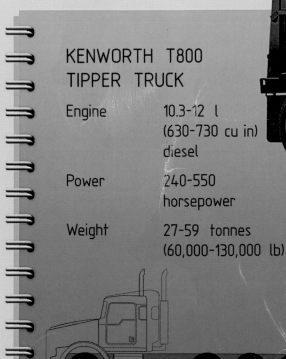

KENWORTH T800
TIPPER TRUCK

Engine	10.3-12 l (630-730 cu in) diesel
Power	240-550 horsepower
Weight	27-59 tonnes (60,000-130,000 lb)

web

FINDER

http://www.macktrucks.com/default.aspx?pageid=210
The history of Mack trucks.
http://www.kenworth.com/brochures/WorkTrucks.pdf
Kenworth trucks, including the T800 tipper truck.

GIANT LIFTERS

When something heavy has to be lifted into place, a truck crane is sometimes brought in for the job. A truck crane is a truck with a crane on top.

ONE TRUCK, TWO CABS

The Terex-Demag AC-200 is a modern truck crane. It has two cabs. The cab at the front is for driving the truck. Another cab further back on one side is for operating the crane. The crane boom is made in seven pieces that slide inside each other to make it small enough to travel on the roads with other traffic.

Boom

Up to eight of the AC-200's 10 wheels can turn to steer round tight bends.

Cab

Cab

TEREX-DEMAG AC-200 TRUCK CRANE

TRUCK ENGINE	516 hp
CRANE ENGINE	231 hp
LENGTH OF BOOM	67.8 m (222 ft)
MAXIMUM LIFT	200 tonnes (441,000 lb)

STAYING UPRIGHT

Before a truck crane like the AC-200 lifts anything, it puts out legs on each side. They are called outriggers and they stop the crane from toppling over. Powerful 'pushers' called hydraulic rams push the boom upwards. The parts of the boom slide out until the boom is the right length.

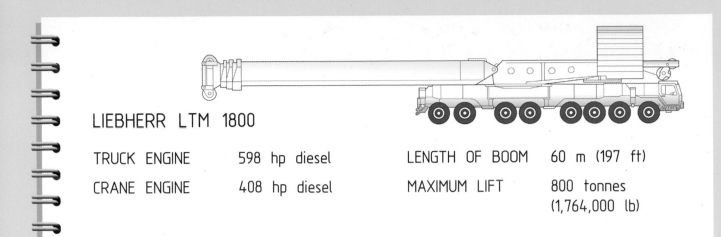

LIEBHERR LTM 1800

TRUCK ENGINE	598 hp diesel	LENGTH OF BOOM	60 m (197 ft)
CRANE ENGINE	408 hp diesel	MAXIMUM LIFT	800 tonnes (1,764,000 lb)

KEEPING YOUR BALANCE

The Liebherr LTM 1800 is a truck crane that can lift loads four times heavier than a 200-tonne crane. A heavy counterweight is fixed at the rear of the crane to enable it to lift heavy loads safely. It balances the weight of the load. The heavier the load to be lifted, the heavier the counterweight used.

web

FINDER

http://www.demag24.com/r_en/prod/ac200-1.aspx
Terex-Demag AC-200 truck crane details.
http://www.liebherr.com/at/en/18739.asp
Information and pictures of the Liebherr LTM 1800 truck crane.

The LTM 1800 has 16 wheels to spread its weight.

MILITARY MOVERS

Armies have to transport very heavy equipment, including tanks. The trucks they use are some of the biggest, heaviest and longest vehicles allowed on public roads.

TRANSPORTING TANKS

The biggest army truck is the Oshkosh M1070 Heavy Equipment Transporter (HET). It pulls the King GTS100 Heavy Equipment Trailer. Together, they can transport a 72-tonne (158,735-lb) battle tank.

The Oshkosh HET transports the US Army's M1 Abrams tanks.

SPREADING THE WEIGHT

The HET and its trailer are so heavy that they could sink into soft ground. To stop them getting stuck, the trailer has a total of 40 wheels to spread the vehicle's great weight over the ground. When the driver turns the tractor's wheels, the trailer's front and back wheels turn too, to help steer this massive vehicle around curves.

The Overland Train's control rig carried a crew of six.

OVERLAND TRAIN

In the 1950s, the US Army needed a big transporter to carry supplies to remote outposts in any climate. One vehicle they tried was the Overland Train. It is still the longest land vehicle ever built. It had a truck called the control rig in front of 12 cargo cars. Each car had four wheels and each wheel was powered by its own electric motor.

LETOURNEAU OVERLAND TRAIN

ENGINE	600 hp diesel
WEIGHT	400 tonnes (880,000 lb)
LENGTH	174 m (572 ft)
CREW	6
TOP SPEED	32 kph (20 mph)

OSHKOSH M1070 HEAVY EQUIPMENT TRANSPORTER AND KING GTS100 HEAVY EQUIPMENT TRAILER

ENGINE	18 l (1,105 cu. in.)
POWER	700 hp
UNLOADED WEIGHT	45 tonnes (99,000 lb)
LOADED WEIGHT	118 tonnes (260,255 lb)

web

FINDER

http://www.oshkoshtruck.com/defense/products~het~1070f.cfm
Find out more about the newest Oshkosh Heavy Equipment Transporter.
http://www.army.mil/fact_files_site/het
Information about the Oshkosh Heavy Equipment Transporter from the US Army.

HEAVY HAULERS

The biggest and heaviest loads need special vehicles to move them. Some are carried on supersized trailers pulled by ordinary trucks, but the most extreme loads need specially designed vehicles.

A Kenworth T800 transports a telescope mirror packed safely inside a steel case.

MOUNTAIN CLIMBING

When, in 2003, a giant mirror had to be delivered to a telescope on top of a mountain, a special vehicle was needed. The mirror was more than 8 metres (27 feet) across. It had to be carried up a steep, narrow and winding road to the Mount Graham International Observatory in Arizona, USA.

BOXING CLEVER

A Kenworth T800 truck was teamed up with a special trailer for the job. The mirror was carried inside a steel box to protect it. The mirror and the box weighed 50 tonnes (110,000 lb). The box was held up on end so that it would fit between the trees at the sides of the narrow road.

KENWORTH T800
HEAVY HAULER

ENGINE	565 hp diesel
WEIGHT CARRIED	82 tonnes (180,000 lb)
SPEED ON MOUNTAIN ROAD	6 kph (4 mph)

SUPER-MOVERS

The most extreme transporters are the crawler-transporters that take space shuttles to the launchpad. Each transporter is 40 metres (131 feet) long and weighs more than 70 normal trucks. Huge diesel engines drive electricity generators that power electric motors. The motors drive eight giant trucks at a slow walking speed.

A crawler-transporter moves the space shuttle Discovery and its launch platform to the launchpad.

NASA CRAWLER-TRANSPORTER

MOTORS	16 electric drive motors
ENGINES	Two 2,750-hp diesel engines
WEIGHT	2,721 tonnes (6,000,000 lb)
TOP SPEED	3 kph (2 mph)

web

FINDER

http://www.kenworth.com/ 6100_pre_mor.asp?file=1494
Read the story of the mirror's journey to the Mount Graham Observatory.
http://science.ksc.nasa.gov/ facilities/crawler.html
Details of NASA's giant crawler-transporters.

BIG-RIGS

PETERBILT MODEL 379 BIG-RIG

ENGINE	14.6 l (890 cu in) diesel
POWER	350-625 hp
UNLOADED WEIGHT	13.6 tonnes (20,000 lb)
LOADED WEIGHT	36 tonnes (80,000 lb)

The Peterbilt Model 379 is a popular truck throughout the world.

The biggest trucks you'll see on most roads are called big-rigs in the United States, semis in Australia, and articulated lorries or 'artics' in the UK.

A CLASSIC BIG-RIG

The Peterbilt Model 379 is a popular big-rig on American highways. The front part is called the tractor. It pulls a semi-trailer carrying the cargo. The tractor and semi-trailer are connected by a part called the fifth wheel. It lets the tractor and semi-trailer swivel. It also lets the tractor unhook one load and pick up another load quickly.

ENGINE POWER

The Peterbilt Model 379's long nose houses a powerful diesel engine. Tall pipes standing up on each side are exhaust pipes. They get rid of waste gases from the engine. Big mirrors stick out from the doors to let the driver see behind. A grille at the front lets air rush in to cool the engine.

KENWORTH T2000 BIG-RIG

ENGINE	11-14 l (670-850 cu in) diesel
POWER	435-600 horsepower
UNLOADED WEIGHT	13.6 tonnes (30,000 lb)
LOADED WEIGHT	36 tonnes (80,000 lb)

The Kenworth T2000 has one of the most streamlined truck bodies.

A SLEEK, SLIPPERY BIG-RIG

The Kenworth T2000 is a new type of big-rig. Its body is designed to slip through the air more easily than older trucks. The body is sleek and gently curving, so that air flows more smoothly around it as well as about the trailer behind it. The sloping nose also gives the driver a clearer view of the road.

web

FINDER

http://www.peterbilt.com/index_gal_mod_desc.asp?model=model379
Find out more about the Peterbilt Model 379 truck.
http://www.kenworth.com/brochures/T2000.pdf
Read about the Kenworth T2000 truck.

LONG HAUL

ROAD TRAIN

Road trains are a common sight in Australia's outback.

The biggest road trucks transport goods and materials across the longest distances. They can't be much wider than other trucks because they have to fit onto ordinary roads, but they are far longer than other trucks.

TRAINS ON THE ROAD

The trucks that transport goods and materials across Australia are so long that they are called road trains. The front part of a road train is a very powerful truck tractor. It has to be powerful because it's pulling such a big, heavy load. In Australia, the tractor is called a prime mover. The prime mover pulls a semi-trailer and at least two more trailers. The longest road trains can have six or more trailers.

FILLING UP WITH FUEL

There are not many fuel stations on the long roads that cross Australia. Road trains have to carry a lot more fuel than other trucks. They have enough fuel for about 1,600 kilometres (1,000 miles).

AUSTRALIAN ROAD TRAIN

ENGINE	650 hp diesel
TRAILERS	3
LENGTH	53 m (174 ft)
LOADED WEIGHT	140 tonnes (308,650 lb)

CENTIPEDE TRUCKS

Most American trucks are not allowed to weigh more than 36 tonnes (80,000 lb), but some states allow heavier trucks. Michigan is famous for its heavyweight trucks. The longest of these trucks have two trailers with lots of wheels. They are known as Michigan Doubles, Michigan Specials, or Michigan Centipedes. They can weigh up to 74 tonnes (164,000 lb).

Michigan trucks are some of the biggest and heaviest on U.S. roads.

MICHIGAN CENTIPEDE

ENGINE	400-500 hp diesel
TRAILERS	2
LENGTH	30 m (100 ft)
LOADED WEIGHT	74 tonnes (164,000 lb)

web

FINDER

http://www.westernstar.com.au
Find out more about Australian road trains.
http://www.ebroadcast.com.au/ecars/Places/Au/Road-Trains.html
Details of Australian road trains.

EMERGENCY!

One of the most important special-purpose trucks is the fire engine. It is designed to carry a team of firefighters and their equipment to a fire as quickly as possible.

WHICH TRUCK'S WHICH?

There are different types of fire engines. Pumper trucks, or pumps, send water out through hoses. Tanker trucks carry extra water. Rescue trucks carry equipment to rescue people trapped in vehicles. Ladder trucks carry ladders firefighters can use to attack a fire from high above the ground. The Seagrave Force 100 is a ladder truck.

TURNTABLE LADDER

The Force 100's ladder extends to a height of 30 metres (100 feet). The ladder stands on a turntable so that it can be turned in any direction. A water hose is fixed to the end of the ladder. Compartments in the truck hold all the equipment the firefighters need, including at least 305 metres (1,000 feet) of hose.

A Seagrave ladder truck belonging to the Fire Department of New York, USA.

An Oshkosh Striker airport fire truck from Washington, USA.

AIRPORT RESCUE

The Oshkosh Striker 4500 is a fire engine specially designed for airports. It can attack a fire with water or foam. Foam is sprayed over spilt fuel to stop it from catching fire. The water or foam is pumped from nozzles, called turrets, on the truck's roof and front bumper.

OSHKOSH STRIKER 4500 FIRE TRUCK

ENGINE	950 hp diesel
TOP SPEED	112 kph (70 mph)
WATER TANK	17,033 l
FOAM TANK	2,385 l

SEAGRAVE FORCE 100 FIRE TRUCK

ENGINE	525 hp diesel
LADDER HEIGHT	30 m (100 ft)
WATER TANK	1,890 l

web

FINDER

http://www.chevroncars.com/wocc/lrn/artcl/artcl.jhtml?id=/content/Car_Corner/a0416.xml
Find out about fire engines.
http://www.seagrave.com/Products/Aerials/Force/Force.html
Details of Seagrave Force fire engines.
http://www.oshkoshtruck.com/airportmunicipal/home.cfm
Meet the Striker airport fire engine.

SPORT TRUCKS

A racing pick-up truck hugs the ground as it rounds a turn.

Trucks make surprisingly good racing vehicles. Small pick-up trucks and even big-rig tractors take part in truck races.

PICK-UP RACING

Pick-up trucks, or utility trucks, are small, open-back trucks about the same size as a car. Pick-ups used for racing look like ordinary road trucks, but they are specially built for racing. They are lighter, more powerful and faster than ordinary trucks. They are also designed to be safer at racing speeds. The driver is protected by a strong metal frame that goes all around the driver's cab.

NASCAR CRAFTSMAN
RACING PICK-UP TRUCK

ENGINE	5.8 l (358 cu. in.)
POWER	700 hp
WEIGHT	1,540 kg (3,400 lb)
TOP SPEED	300 kph (190 mph)

CHANGING SHAPE

The open back of an ordinary pick-up truck 'catches' a lot of air and slows the truck down. This doesn't matter for a road truck, but it would slow down a racing truck too much. So, the back of a racing pick-up is covered to give it a smoother shape. This helps it to slip through the air faster.

SUPER TRUCKS

Super Trucks are big-rig tractors with super-powerful engines. Like racing pick-ups, Super Trucks are specially built for the race track. Compared to the ordinary trucks you see on the roads, these racing machines are stronger, more streamlined, and more than twice as powerful.

SUPER TRUCK
RACING TRUCK

ENGINE	11.1 l (680 cu in) diesel
POWER	1,000 hp
WEIGHT	5,800 kg (12,800 lb)
TOP SPEED	160 kph (100 mph)

Super Truck racing engines are twice as powerful as standard truck engines.

web

FINDER

http://www.worldofmotorsport.com/pickups.php
Find out more about pick-up truck racing.
http://www.tricklefan.com/manual/div_truck.html
Read about NASCAR Craftsman Truck racing in the United States.
http://trucktrend.com/roadtests/ultimate/163_0402_trkracing
Pictures and information about Super Truck racing.

MONSTERS

Monster trucks are specially built trucks with very big wheels. They entertain crowds of spectators at special events by racing, jumping in the air, and crushing other vehicles by driving over them.

Changing a tyre on Bigfoot 5 is a mammoth task!

BIGFOOT 5 MONSTER TRUCK

ENGINE	7.5 l (460 cu in)
HEIGHT	4.7 m (15 ft 6 in)
WEIGHT (with 4 tyres)	12,700 kg (28,000 lb)
WEIGHT (with 8 tyres)	17,240 kg (38,000 lb)

THE BIGGEST MONSTER

The biggest monster truck is called Bigfoot 5. The truck's body is dwarfed by its giant wheels. The tyres were made for the US Army's Overland Train *(see page 13)*. Each tyre stands 3 metres (10 feet) high and weighs as much as a small car!

DOUBLE TROUBLE

When Bigfoot 5 made its first appearance in 1986, it had twice the normal number of wheels. It had four giant wheels at the front and four at the back. It instantly became the world's tallest, widest and heaviest monster truck, records it still holds today.

WE HAVE LIFT-OFF!

Monster trucks are famous for their amazing stunts, including jumping over other vehicles. In 1999, Bigfoot 14 jumped over a Boeing 727 airliner. It set two records. As it headed towards the jump, it reached a world record speed for a monster truck – of 111.5 kph (69.3 mph). It also set the record for the longest-ever monster truck jump – a distance of 61.5 metres (202 feet).

FINDER

http://www.bigfoot4x4.com/bf5.html
Read about Bigfoot 5.
http://www.bigfoot4x4.com/bf14.html
Bigfoot 14's page.

BIGFOOT 14 MONSTER TRUCK

ENGINE	9.4 l (572 cu. in.)
HEIGHT	3 m (10 ft)
WEIGHT	4,535 kg (10,000 lb)

Bigfoot 14 has wowed the crowds with its amazing jumps since 1994.

FUTURE FREIGHTERS

Truck companies are always thinking about what future trucks might be like. They try out new ideas by making vehicles called 'concept' trucks. Ideas that work well are then built into trucks in the future.

CURVY CAB

The Renault Radiance concept truck shows that trucks don't have to look dull. Most trucks are square and box-shaped, but the Radiance has a more curvy, streamlined body. The driver's cab has big windows to give a good view. Cameras built into the truck's body show spots that are hard for the driver to see.

SMART INSIDE

The inside of the driver's cab is very futuristic. The driver uses a smart card instead of a key to get into the cab and start the engine. The cab looks like a modern office.

RENAULT RADIANCE

BODY	Streamlined shape
FEATURES	Smart-card entry
	Foldaway gear lever
	Mirrors replaced by cameras
	Windows can be darkened

The streamlined shape of the Radiance means it burns less fuel.

The Mercedes Ext-92's wraparound windscreen gives the driver a very clear view.

SAVING FUEL

The Mercedes Ext-92 (European Experimental Truck) was designed in 1992, but it still looks very futuristic today. Its amazing shape is designed to let it slip through air very easily. Just changing a truck's shape like this saves fuel, and that makes the truck less expensive to run.

MERCEDES EXT-92

BODY   Fully streamlined shape

FEATURES   Smart-card entry

               Mirrors replaced by cameras

               Radar warns of vehicles too close

               Driver's seat in the centre

               Windows can be darkened

web

FINDER

http://www.cardesignnews.com/news/2004/041220renault-radiance
See more pictures of the Renault Radiance.
http://www.germancarfans.com/news.cfm/newsid/2041231.002/page/2/mercedes/1.html
Read about the Mercedes Ext-92 concept truck.

TIMELINE

1769
French military engineer Nicolas Cugnot builds a steam-powered tractor. It is the first vehicle to move under its own power. A second tractor built by Cugnot in 1770 still exists today.

1861
German engineer Nikolaus Otto builds a new type of petrol engine. It is the first practical alternative to the steam engine.

1885
German engineer Karl Benz builds the world's first practical automobile powered by a petrol engine. It is a three-wheeler with a top speed of about 13 kph (8 mph).

1801
British engineer Richard Trevithick builds a steam-powered carriage.

1862
Belgian inventor Étienne Lenoir builds the first successful internal combustion engine and also the first vehicle powered by an internal combustion engine.

1887
German engineers Gottlieb Daimler and Wilhelm Maybach produce the first four-wheel automobile powered by an internal combustion engine. It had been built originally as a horse-drawn carriage.

1829
The first steam-powered fire engines are invented by John Braithwaite and John Ericsson in London, England. At first they are unpopular, because they take work away from people who operate hand-powered water pumps. Other people think they are not powerful enough.

1862
The public see three steam-powered fire engines on display at the International Exhibition held in Hyde Park, London.

1888
Scotsman John Boyd Dunlop invents the pneumatic (air-filled) rubber tyre. It was used on bicycles first, but pneumatic tyres were later fitted to larger vehicles, including trucks.

1858
The first successful steam-powered fire engine starts work. Soon, the 'steamers' can pump water faster than hand-operated fire pumps.

1863
Ten steam-powered fire engines, seven British and three American, take part in a three-day trial at Crystal Palace, London. An engine built by the British Merryweather company wins.

1889
Daimler and Maybach build the first automobile that is designed from the start as an automobile.

1892

French engineer Rudolf Diesel invents a new type of engine, called a diesel engine, that will later power most trucks.

1896

The Daimler Phoenix 1.5-tonner becomes the world's first petrol-engine truck.

1897

Rudolf Diesel builds the first practical diesel engine. The 25-hp engine is simple and works well. It soon becomes very popular, making Diesel very wealthy.

1903

The first petrol fire engines start work in London.

1913

Trucks are fitted with wheels that can be replaced. Trucks start carrying spare wheels.

1914

The first wrecker (recovery truck) is built in the United States.

1914

American August Fruehauf builds the first articulated truck from a tractor unit pulling a separate semi-trailer.

1925

Pneumatic (air-filled) truck tyres begin to replace solid rubber tyres.

1930

The first diesel-engine trucks are built. They begin to replace steam-powered trucks and petrol-engine trucks.

1950

Most large trucks – such as the one below – are now powered by diesel engines.

1951

Power steering makes it easier to turn the steering wheels of heavy vehicles such as trucks.

1954

Standard sizes of freight containers are introduced.

1983

The heaviest trucks allowed on British roads are set at 38 tonnes (83,800 lb).

1992

Mercedes unveils its futuristic Ext-92 concept truck.

2004

Renault shows its Radiance concept truck in Hanover, Germany.

GLOSSARY

ARTICULATED TRUCK

A truck with a tractor pulling a semi-trailer.

BOOM

A crane's arm, also called a jib.

CENTIPEDE

A very long and heavy truck with lots of wheels. Centipedes are common in the US state of Michigan.

CONCEPT TRUCK

A truck built to show how future trucks might look. 'Concept' means idea.

COUNTERWEIGHT

A heavy weight hung from one side of a truck crane to balance the load being lifted by the crane, so that the truck does not fall over.

CU IN

Cubic inch – a small space measuring one inch long, one inch wide, and one inch high. The size of an engine is measured in cubic inches.

DIESEL ENGINE

A type of engine that powers most trucks. A diesel engine burns an oily fuel called diesel oil. Both of them are named after the man who invented the engine, Rudolf Diesel.

FIFTH WHEEL

The part of an articulated truck, or 'big-rig', where the tractor (the front part) is joined to the semi-trailer (the back part).

FREIGHT

Transported goods.

GENERATOR

A machine for making electricity.

HORSEPOWER (HP)

A unit of power. The power of an engine is measured in horsepower. A small family car might have an engine up to about 150 horsepower. Most trucks have engines of 300-600 horsepower.

INTERNAL COMBUSTION ENGINE

A type of engine. Its fuel (petrol or diesel oil) is burned inside the engine instead of in a separate furnace. A modern truck engine is an internal combustion engine.

KPH

Kilometre per hour – a unit of speed. A truck travelling at 40 kph takes one hour to go a distance of 40 kilometres. 40 kph is about the same speed as 25 miles per hour.

MONSTER TRUCK

A truck with huge wheels, built for racing, jumping and crushing other vehicles to entertain crowds.

MPH

Miles per hour – a measurement of speed. A truck travelling at 25 mph takes one hour to go a distance of 25 miles. 25 mph is about the same speed as 40 kilometres per hour.

NASA

The National Aeronautics and Space Administration – the organisation responsible for non-military space research and space flights in the United States.

PICK-UP TRUCK

A small type of truck with an open back for carrying goods and materials. Also called a utility truck or 'ute'.

PRIME MOVER

Another name for a truck tractor in Australia.

ROAD TRAIN

A very long truck made from a tractor pulling a semi-trailer and at least two more trailers. Road trains transport goods and materials in Australia.

SEMI-TRAILER

The back part of an articulated truck. The semi-trailer is pulled by the tractor. It's called a semi-trailer because it has no wheels at the front. The front rests on the back of the tractor.

STEAM ENGINE

An engine worked by steam. Fuel (wood or coal) burned in a furnace heats water in a boiler. The water makes steam and the steam makes the engine go.

STEAM TRUCK

A truck powered by a steam engine. Also called a 'steamer'. Many trucks were steamers up to the 1930s.

STREAMLINED

Shaped to move through air easily. A streamlined truck has a smooth, gently curving body.

TONNE

A unit of weight, also called a metric ton. A tonne is the same as 1,000 kilograms, or about 2,205 pounds. The ton can be a confusing unit to use, because there are several different 'tons'. A British ton, or long ton, is equal to 2,240 pounds. An American short ton is equal to 2,000 pounds. A metric ton, or tonne, is equal to 1,000 kilograms, or about 2,205 pounds

TRACTOR

A vehicle that pulls a machine, trailer or semi-trailer. Farm tractors pull all sorts of machines for working on the land and dealing with crops. A truck tractor pulls a semi-trailer.

INDEX